COZY
COTTAGE DECOR

Grayscale Coloring Book For Adults

...By...

Gladys Holmes

This book belong to:

....

....

How to use this book...

Consider placing a sheet of paper behind the page
you are coloring to prevent bleed-through or smudging.

Coloring Tips & Techniques...

1. Choose the right kind of color, so pick the one that suits your preference and project such as colored pencils, markers, watercolors, acrylics, digital tools, etc.

2. Practice Blending: Blending colors together can create beautiful gradients and smoother transitions.

3. Explore Color Theory: Understanding color theory can help you create harmonious and visually appealing color combinations. Learn about primary, secondary, and tertiary colors, complementary colors, analogous colors, etc.

4. Start with Light Colors: Begin coloring with light shades and gradually build up the intensity. This allows you to correct mistakes easily.

5. Use Reference Images: If you're coloring a specific subject (e.g., animals, landscapes, portraits), refer to real-life images or photographs to understand how colors work in real scenarios.

6. Enjoy the coloring: Lastly, remember that coloring is a relaxation. Don't be too critical of yourself, and **ENJOY COLORING!**

30719982R00064